THE BIGGS BOOK of Organ Music

Edited and Arranged
by
E. POWER BIGGS

with Hammond Registrations
by
CHESTER KINGSBURY and PORTER HEAPS

CONTENTS

E. POWER BIGGS
(March 29, 1906 - March 10, 1977)

A COLLEAGUE'S TRIBUTE

British born and British trained, he adopted us and we adopted him. I know of no other person who has done as much for organ music the world over as E. Power Biggs. Coming to this country early in his career, he became a United States citizen in 1937, eventually settling in Cambridge, Massachusetts. He may seldom have been "in residence" there, however, because of his many concert tours and recordings.

Biggs achieved eminence in five fields: concerts, recordings, broadcasts, editing and arranging, and organ design. His concerts took him all over Europe and America. He was in demand for performances with orchestras and for appearances with instrumental ensembles. His playing was always crisp, clear and rhythmic. He achieved his results by careful attention to articulation rather than to color. Registration was conceived on a broad scale, probably because of his experience in recording. His taste in repertoire was eclectic, but he did not venture into the experimentation of the extreme avant-garde. His interest in, and performance of, new compositions for organ encouraged U.S. composers to write for the instrument.

In his many recordings he made available a wealth of music, much of which had not been recorded before. His penchant for recording the same composition on many European organs did much to acquaint U.S. organists with the unique tone quality of these historic instruments. In addition to solo organ works, he recorded many compositions with various instrumental ensembles. Here, as in his concerts, the repertoire covers a wide range of interest – from Gabrieli and Telemann to Aaron Copland and Scott Joplin!

His Sunday morning broadcasts from the Germanic Museum (later renamed The Busch-Reisinger Museum of Germanic Culture) at Harvard extended from 1942 to 1958. These live broadcasts, devoted to the whole gamut of solo and ensemble literature, did much to promote an interest in organ music.

In his editing and arranging he made available – in practical editions – much music that was not easily accessible. Here he did much to enrich the literature, using the organ in instrumental ensembles.

Biggs, G. Donald Harrison and Walter Holtkamp were the ones who began the renaissance in organ building in this country. Builders became aware of the authentic tone of the best European instruments. Largely as a result of the pioneering efforts of these three men, the best U.S. companies now build organs according to classic design.

He was genial and friendly. I never heard him make disparaging remarks about his colleagues, although I am sure he did disapprove of much that was being done to make organ music "attractive". Only by the example of his serious devotion to the music itself did he emphasize the difference between real artistry and showmanship. Our friend "Biggsie" is no longer with us, but his influence continues to live.

LESLIE P. SPELMAN
La Jolla, California

BIOGRAPHICAL SKETCHES

... the early years

Edward Power Biggs was born March 29, 1906 at Cranleigh Road, Westcliff-on-Sea, Essex County, east of London on the Thames Estuary. His parents were Alice Maude (Tredgett) Biggs and Clarence Power Biggs. His father was an auctioneer and his mother was a nurse.

In 1907 the family moved to Ventnor, Isle of Wight, to a rambling Victorian house, Highport Towers*. EPB's father had tuberculosis, and EPB's mother took in paying guests to support the family. When EPB was three years old, his father died, and his mother chose to stay at Highport Towers to maintain herself and her son until EPB completed public school education.

At seven, EPB was accepted at Hurstpierpoint College in Sussex. There he endured an average number of canings, played soccer well, suffered cold hands and feet each winter, and survived the war years with many an evening meal of bread and drippings. In order to get home for holidays, he would walk from school to take a ferry to Cowes or Ryde, and then walk over the downs to Ventnor.

It was at Hurstpierpoint College that he received his first formal musical education. At age seven he began his study of the piano. He enjoyed it, was quick to grasp the fundamentals, and he worked hard for about six years. Then a change of music master, and too many sharp raps on his knuckles, discouraged him from further study.

EPB remembered Armistice Day, 1918, very clearly: church bells ringing, the whistles and noise makers, and the general rejoicing of the day. He remembered because he celebrated that day in the infirmary at Hurstpierpoint in isolation with influenza!

In 1922, at age 16, his education at Hurstpierpoint College completed, he entered into a three year agreement with an electrical engineering firm. This arrangement combined job training with formal instruction. He would work a full day and then attend evening classes and study for written examinations in the evenings. But even with this heavy schedule he returned to music, as part-time organ assistant to J. Stuart Archer in return for instruction.

Archer's influence was important, for he urged EPB to apply for a scholarship at the Royal Academy of Music, London. Archer's second bit of advice was equally as important: if accepted at the Academy, EPB was to study organ with G.D. Cunningham only.

In the spring of 1924, EPB won the Thomas Threlfall organ scholarship at the Academy. He had played the slow movement from Rheinberger's Seventh Sonata – not particularly well, he said. It was just that no one else played better. And then he had to convince his mother and family that the change was necessary and for the best. He had also to be granted a release from his contract with the engineering firm. All these obstacles were finally hurdled, but only on the condition that if he failed at the Academy he was to return immediately to his contract with the firm.

That summer of 1924 was to seem very long, for EPB could not shake the thought that a mistake had been made, and that the scholarship might be withdrawn.

At the Academy he studied organ with G.D. Cunningham, piano with C. Pollard and harmony with J.A. Sowerbutts. He received the Hubert Kiver Organ Prize in 1927, and completed his studies in 1928. A final report from the Warden, H.W. Richards, says "...from the reports I should think Mr. Power Biggs has every possibility of success both inside the Academy and out". But it was Warden Richards who also said that it would be better for EPB to leave the Academy, that he ought not to try for a position as a teaching assistant.

One of EPB's classmates in organ at the Academy, Owen Le.P. Franklin, had toured the United States in 1928-1929. During his tour, Franklin had obtained a church position in the United States, and he looked forward to returning to live in the USA permanently. So EPB was delighted when a similar opportunity came to him. From October 6, 1929 to May 25, 1930, he toured the United States, playing 190 recitals. He was in the company of Rhys Davis, a Welsh singer, and Miss Christine, a soprano. Miss Christine was the wife of David Jones, who organized the tour. All arrangements were made by Jones; but because he kept just about two days ahead of the group, the seven months' trip was full of suspense and surprise. At the end of the tour, neither Davis nor EPB had any money. Nor had EPB obtained even a suggestion of a position as organist; but he went back to England and immediately applied for permanent residence in the United States. This was granted, but only because he had no promise of work. This was 1930! (Franklin, because he had a job, was not permitted to return to the United States.)

On August 23, 1930, EPB again sailed for the USA, armed only with a "To Whom It May Concern"

**In 1970, E. Power Biggs went to Ventnor and found Highport Towers little changed from 1907, although the broad expanse of lawn to the cliffs overlooking the Channel seemed greatly diminished to him, either by sea erosion or by adult perspective and time.*

letter from G.D. Cunningham. As EPB went through customs, the inspector examined the luggage quite carefully; he asked what the wands (the batons) were for, and why EPB wished to live in the United States. EPB explained that he was a musician, and that he had come because he liked the country. At this, the customs officer slammed shut the trunk, and wished the new arrival the very best of luck. Dr. T. Tertius Noble helped him find a position in 1930 at Emmanuel Church, Newport, Rhode Island, where he remained until he went to Christ Church, Cambridge, in 1932. In September of 1937 he received his United States citizenship, and Cambridge became his permanent home.

PEGGY BIGGS
Cambridge, Massachusetts

.... the later years

It is difficult to say which of the many aspects of E. Power Biggs's career contributed the most to his popularity as a performer. Certainly the weekly solo programs over CBS made him known to millions of people in the United States and in other countries. From 1942-1958, these programs were broadcast coast to coast, to Alaska, and by short wave to Europe.

His concert tours took him to all the major universities in the USA and to churches all across the country. Foreign tours included concerts in Australia, Iceland, Mexico City, England and most of continental Europe. Important in bringing the literature for Organ and Orchestra to the attention of a wide audience were his appearances with the Boston Symphony Orchestra, the Philadelphia, the New York Philharmonic, the BBC Orchestra, the London Philharmonic Orchestra, the Royal Liverpool Philharmonic Orchestra, the Mozarteum Orchestra in Salzburg, and many others. In these appearances, E. Power Biggs played the first performances of many of the major works for Organ and Orchestra.

Both in Europe and America, the medium of television brought his artistry to millions more. Of particular interest were the programs featuring the music of Scott Joplin played on a Pedal Harpsichord; from Switzerland, a program on the oldest organ in the world – built in 1390; and a film on Johann Sebastian Bach made during EPB's last visit to Leipzig.

Biggs contributed many articles to such periodicals as "Horizon", "Saturday Review", "High Fidelity", etc. But no articles can contribute as much to the understanding of all the artistry and wide interest of this man as do the many, many recordings he has left the musical world.

Of these many recordings, perhaps none can be said to add as much to the understanding of Organs and Organ Literature as the "Historic Organ" series, which brings to the listener the sounds of historic organs in Europe and America. It was during the last twenty-five years of his life that Biggs devoted his attention to these old organs, and as a result, he probably knew more about them than anyone else.

THE PUBLISHER

HONORS

Elected Fellow of the American Academy of Arts and Sciences
Fellow (hon.) Royal Academy of Music, London
Fellow (hon.) Royal College of Organists, London
Mus. Doc. (hon.) Acadia University, Nova Scotia
Mus. Doc. (hon.) New England Conservatory of Music
Doctor of Fine Arts (hon.) Coe College, Iowa

Citation for services to American Music, National Association of American Composers and Conductors

Knight-Commander: Orden de Isabel la Catolica, awarded for research and furthering of interest in historic Spanish organs and organ music.

ADAGIO
(For the Glass Harmonica or Musical Glasses)

Soft Flute stops
or Celesta

by
WOLFGANG AMADEUS MOZART
(K. 356)

Arranged for Organ Solo by
E. POWER BIGGS

Hammond Registration
(in frames) by
CHESTER KINGSBURY

Sw.	A♯	00 6231 000
	B	00 4211 000
Gt.	A♯	00 8443 000

Vibrato: OFF

Prepare: Sw. A♯ Gt. A♯

Mozart wrote this short movement for the Glass Harmonica, an instrument consisting of a set of rotating Musical Glasses, improved and perfected by Benjamin Franklin. Performance is appropriate on the light Flute stops of an Organ, or on the Celesta.

Sw. A♯
Sw.
As at first
Gt.
Solo Flute
Sw. B

Sw. A♯
Sw.
As at first
Reduce
Sw. B
pp
rall.

ALL GLORY BE TO GOD ON HIGH

(Allein Gott in der Höh' sei Ehr')

Festival Prelude for Organ

Sw. Full, with Mixtures
Gt. Full, with Mixtures, Sw. & Ch. to Gt.
Ch. Full, with Mixtures
Ped. Full, with Mixtures

Hammond Registration (in Circles and Frames) by PORTER HEAPS
Gt. [A#] 66 7858 666
Pedal 8-6 Vibrato: Off

JOHANN SEBASTIAN BACH
Arranged by E. Power Biggs

Broadly (♩= 48) (*interludes with freedom*)

**On Hammond, play both hands an octave higher.*

cresc.
rall.

ANDANTE

(From Concerto No. 3 in B-flat)

by

WILLIAM FELTON*

Arranged by

E. POWER BIGGS

Gt. Flutes, 8′ & 4′
Sw. Salicional 8′, Flute 4′ uncoupled
Ch. soft 8′, 4′
Ped. 16′, 8′

Hammond Registration (in Frames) by CHESTER KINGSBURY

Sw.	A#	00 3745 343	
	B	00 5225 001	
Gt.	A#	00 6826 030	
	B	00 5225 001	

Pedal 3-3 Vibrato: OFF
Prepare; Sw. A# Gt. A#

The Rev. William Felton, Scholar at Cambridge, Vicar-Choral of Hereford Cathedral in 1741, and Chaplain to the Princess Dowager of Wales. The Concerto is scored for organ with string orchestra and Oboes.

Gt.
Gt.
Ch.
Sw. B
Sw. A♯
Sw.
Sw.
Sw.
Gt. B
Ch.
Gt. A♯
Gt.
Gt. B
Ch.
Sw.
Sw.
Gt. A♯
Gt.
Ch.
Gt. B
Sw.
Sw.
Gt. A♯
Gt.
Sw. B
Ch.

Gt.
Gt.
Sw.A♯
Sw.
Sw.B
Ch.
tr
Gt.
Gt.
Sw.
Sw.A♯
Ch.
Sw.B
Gt.
Gt.
Sw.A♯
Sw.
rall.

Prelude on "AVE VERUM CORPUS"

by
WOLFGANG AMADEUS MOZART

Arranged for Organ Solo by
E. POWER BIGGS

Sw. Salicional 8′, Flute 4′, Oboe (or Solo English Horn)
Gt. Full to 2′
Ch. 8′, 4′ accompanimental stops
Ped. 16′, 8′, Ch. to Ped.

Hammond Registration (in frames) by CHESTER KINGSBURY

Sw.	A♯	00 4885 430
	B	00 2763 210
Gt.	A♯	21 6636 035
	B	00 5325 000
Ped.	4-2	Vibrato: OFF
Prepare:		Sw. B Gt. B

Mozart's famous Motet "AVE VERUM CORPUS" was foreshadowed two years before in this Adagio movement for English Horn and Strings. Transferred to the Organ, the music may be regarded as a "Prelude on AVE VERUM CORPUS."

Sw. F♯
add
Gt. E
add
Ped. 4 - 3
Ped. 4 - 2

Sw. B
reduce
Gt. B
Sw.
Sw.
Gt. A♯
Gt. f
mf Gt. B
Ch.
Gt. A♯
Gt. f
Ped. 5-3
Ped. 4-2
Ped. 5-3
Sw.
Sw.
mf Gt. B
Ch.
Ped. 4-2

Adjust Gt. A♯:
00 6636 000
Sw. A♯

Sw.
Sw. G#
Gt. A#
Ped. 4 - 3
Ped. 5 - 3
add
f
Sw. A#
Ped. 4 - 3
Sw. B
Gt. B
reduce
mf
Ped. 4 - 2

A CHRISTMAS PASTORALE

From The Christmas Concerto by
GIUSEPPE VALENTINI
(1680 - ?)

Arranged for Organ Solo by
E. POWER BIGGS

Sw. Soft acc. stops
Gt. Flute 8′
Ch. Clarinet
Ped. Soft 16′ 8′

Hammond Registration
(in frames) by
CHESTER KINGSBURY

Sw. A♯ 00 3523 000
B 00 7520 000
Gt. A♯ 00 5060 640
B 00 3523 000
Ped. 4 - 2 Vibrato: OFF

Prepare: Sw. A♯ Gt. A♯

Sw. A♯
Sw.
p
Sw. B
Gt.
mf
Sw.
Gt. B
Gt. A♯
Ch.
Gt.
Ch.
Sw. A♯
Sw.
Sw.
Gt.
cresc.
Sw. B
Gt.

Sw.
Gt.
f
Ch.
Gt.
Gt.
Ch.
mf
Gt.
Sw.
Gt. B
Sw.
p
Ped. 4-5
add Ch. to Ped.
Very slowly
Sw.
Gt.
Gt. A♯
Ch.
Gt.
Sw.
rall.
pp
ppp
Sw. A♯
Ped. 4-2
Ch. to Ped. off

THE CUCKOO

by

LOUIS CLAUDE D'AQUIN

Arranged for Organ by

E. POWER BIGGS

Gt. (or Solo) Solo Flute (*mf*)
Ch. Flutes 8', 2' (*p*)

Hammond Registration by
CHESTER KINGSBURY

Sw. B   00 4013 000
Gt. B   00 7132 000
Vibrato: OFF

Prepare: Sw. B   Gt. B

Gt. Gt.
Sw. Ch.
Gt. Gt.
Sw. Ch.

Gt. Gt.
Sw. Ch.
Gt. Gt.
Sw. Ch.
Gt. Gt.

Sw. Ch.

Gt. Gt.
Sw. Ch.
Gt.

Sw.
Gt. Gt.
Sw. Ch.
rall.

For Lilo and José Montes-Baquer

THE EMPEROR'S FANFARE
(from Sixth Double Concerto)

ANTONIO SOLER
(1729 - 1783)

Freely adapted, arranged and titled by
E. POWER BIGGS

Hammond Registration
(in Frames) by
CHESTER KINGSBURY
Sw. A# 00 4868 430
Gt. A# 13 7888 763
Pedal 6-5 Vibrato OFF
Prepare: Sw. A# Gt. A#

Man. II
Sw.
f

Man. I
Gt.
Man. I
Gt.
Man. II
Sw.
Man. I
Gt.
Man. I
Gt.
ff

rall.

Pastorale "THE FAITHFUL SHEPHERD
(Il Pastor Fido)

GEORGE FREDERICK HANDEL

Arranged for Organ by
E. POWER BIGGS

Sw. Oboe
Gt. Full to 15th
Ch. Flutes
Ped. 16′, 8′, Ch. to Ped.

Hammond Registration
(in frames) by
CHESTER KINGSBURY

Sw.	A♯	00	3655	100
	B	11	5745	012
Gt.	A♯	00	4522	000
	B	00	4644	011

Ped. 4-2 Vibrato: OFF
Prepare: Sw. A♯ Gt. A♯

With an easy flow

L.H. Sw.
Sw.
cresc.
f
p Ch.
Gt.
f L.H. Sw.
Sw.
p

rall.
a tempo
L.H. Sw.
Sw.
Sw.
Gt.
Gt. f
Sw. B
Ped. 5-3
(Gt. to Ped.)
rall.
Gt.
Ch. p
a tempo
Gt.
Ch.
Ped. 4-3
(Gt. to Ped. off)
Prep. Sw. A♯

L.H. Sw.
Sw.
rall.
a tempo
Ped. 4 - 2
Gt. B
add to Ch. mf
L.H. Ch.
Gt.
Ped. 4-4
Gt. A♯
reduce Ch. pp
L.H. Sw.
Sw.
rall.
Ped. 4-2

THE FIFERS

by

FRANÇOIS DANDRIEU

Arranged for Organ by

E. POWER BIGGS

HAMMOND REGISTRATION BY
CHESTER KINGSBURY

Sw. A♯ 00 5000 000
B 00 8225 023
Gt. A♯ 00 5003 001
B 00 6014 012
Vibrato: OFF

Prepare: Sw. D Gt. A♯

Sw. Salicional 8′, Flute 4′
Gt. Flute 8′, 2′
Ch. Flute 8′, 2′

Sw. B
Gt.
Gt.
Ch.
Gt. A♯
Ch. (as at first)
p
Sw. D
Sw. pp
Sw. A♯
Ch. 8′ only
pp
Gt. D
Sw. Salicional 8′ only
dim.

FIREWORK MUSIC

Hammond Registration
(in Circles and Frames) by
PORTER HEAPS

Sw.	(A♯)	00 4422 221
	(B)	00 5765 420
Gt.	[A♯]	00 3504 004
	[B]	33 6646 555
Pedal 5-4		Vibrato: OFF

Sw.
Gt. } Full, with Mixtures,
Ch. } Sw. & Ch. to Gt.
Ped. Full, with Mixtures

Composed for the Firework display given in Green Park, London, on April 27th, 1749, in celebration of the Peace of Aix-la-Chapelle. The original orchestration is for wind instruments.

1. Overture

GEORGE FREDERICK HANDEL
Arranged by E. Power Biggs

Gt.
Gt.
Ch.
Sw.
Gt.
Gt.
Ch.
Sw.
Gt.
Gt.
ff

Full Organ with Reeds

2. The Rejoicing

Sw. (G♯) (00 6876 540)*
Gt. [F] (00 5652 200)
Pedal 5 - 4

**As the pre-set combinations vary on some models, the intended registration is given in parentheses.*

Gt.
Sw.
rit.

Sw. Strings 8′
Gt. Flute 8′
Ch. Strings 8′, Sw. to Ch.
Ped. soft 16′, Sw. to Ped.

3. The Peace

Sw. (A♯) Vibrato: 1 (slow)
Gt. [G♯] (00 8040 000)
Ped. 3-2

Ch.
Sw.
Gt.
Gt.
Sw.
Sw.
rit.

Sw. 8′, 2′
Gt. 8′, 2′, Sw. to Gt.
Ch. 8′, 2′ only

4. Bourree

Sw. (D) (00 4432 000)
Gt. [A#]
Vibrato: OFF

With animation

Full Organ with Reeds

5. Minuet Finale

Sw. (G) (00 5644 320)
Gt. [B]
Pedal 5-4 Vibrato: OFF

With strong rhythm

tr
Gt.
Gt.
ff
rit.

Sw. Full, with Mixtures, Reeds 8′ & 4′
Gt. Full, with Mixtures, Sw. & Ch. to Gt.
Ch. Full, Sw. to Ch.
Ped. Full, Sw., Gt. & Ch. to Ped.

FUGUE IN C MAJOR
(The "Fanfare" Fugue)

Hammond Registration
(in Circles and Frames) by
PORTER HEAPS
Sw. Ⓑ 00 7655 443
Gt. [B] 33 7866 666
Pedal (to balance) Vibrato: OFF

JOHANN SEBASTIAN BACH
Arranged by E. Power Biggs

Brilliantly (♩= about 72)

Ch. (stay on Gt.)
Ch.
Sw.
rall. cresc.

a tempo
Gt.
Gt.
ff
Full Ped.
tr.
tr
Freely
Full
rall.

GOD'S TIME IS THE BEST
(Sinfonia to Cantata No. 106)

by
J. S. BACH

Arranged for Organ Solo by
E. POWER BIGGS

Hammond Registration
(in frames) by
CHESTER KINGSBURY

Sw. A♯ 00 4251 400
B 00 6251 100
Gt. A♯ 00 4113 001
Pedal 3 - 2 Vibrato: **OFF**
(or ad lib.)

Prepare: Sw. B Gt. A♯

tr
Sw. A♯
Sw. B
Sw. A♯
Sw. B
Sw. A♯
Sw. B
tr
rall.

I STAND AT THE THRESHOLD (Arioso)

(Sinfonia to Cantata No. 156)

J. S. BACH

Arranged for Organ Solo by

E. POWER BIGGS

Hammond Registration
(in frames) by
CHESTER KINGSBURY

Sw. A# 00 0662 400
Gt. A# 00 3414 100
Pedal 3-2 Vibrato: OFF
(or ad lib.)
Prepare: Sw. A# Gt. A#

Slowly and expressively

Sw. A♯
Gt. A♯
Ped. 3-2

JESU, JOY OF MAN'S DESIRING
(from Cantata No. 147)

Manual I - Solo Reed Stop or Combination
Manual II - Flutes 8′ and 4′
Pedal - 16′ and 8′ to Manual II

JOHANN SEBASTIAN BACH

Arranged for Organ Solo by
E. POWER BIGGS

Hammond Registration by
CHESTER KINGSBURY

Sw. A♯	00	5612	000
B	00	6724	011
Gt. B	00	8585	651
Ped.	4-2	Vibrato: OFF	

Prepare: Sw. A♯ Gt. D♯

Also published for: Piano and Organ Duet; and for Three Trumpets and Organ.

Man. II
Sw.
Gt.
Man. I
Sw.
Man. II
Sw.
(Man. II)
Man. I
Gt.

Man. II
Sw.
Gt.
Man. I
Man. II
Sw.
Prepare Gt. B
Ped. 5-3
Sw. B
add to Man. II
Gt.
Man. I (add)

Sw.
Man. II
Gt.
Man. I
Sw.
Man. II
3
3
Gt.
Man. I
Sw.
A#
reduce
3
3

Sw.
Man. II
Gt D♯
Man. I (reduce)
Ped 4-2
Man II
Sw.
rall.

THE MUSICAL CLOCKS
(Flötenuhr)

Arranged by
E. POWER BIGGS

The Music by
FRANZ JOSEF HAYDN

These pieces are from a set of twelve written in 1792 by Haydn for a famous clock in Vienna. They were played automatically on a small flute organ, operated by the clock mechanism.

Hammond Registration
(in Frames)

Sw. B 00 7046 000
Gt. A♯ 00 7225 000
B 00 8347 034

Pedal 4–5 Vibrato: OFF

I. Minuet (Song of the Quail)

II. March

III. Andantino

OFFERTOIRE FOR EASTER
On the Melody "O Filii et Filiae"
(Ye Sons and Daughters of the King)

Hammond Registration
(in Circles and Frames) by
PORTER HEAPS

Sw.	(A#)	00 5250 301
	(B)	00 3500 040
Gt.	[A#]	00 4522 222
	[B]	22 5545 445

Pedal 5 - 4 Vibrato: OFF

Arranged for Organ by
E. POWER BIGGS

FRANÇOIS DANDRIEU

O Filii et Filiae

15th Century French Melody, with Alleluias

(G) (00 5644 320)*

VARIATIONS

**As the pre-set combinations vary on some models, the intended registration is given in parentheses.*

*To facilitate changing drawbar registrations, it is suggested that the final notes in the left hand in each variation be played with the Pedals.

†(F) = 00 5403 000

(Gt. to Mixture)
Gt.
Gt.
f
Ch. to Mixture
B
mf
(detached)
Sw. Oboe

Gt.
A♯
(Sw.)
(Ped.)
Ch. 8′, 2′
A♯
00 5200 301
p
Ch.
simile

(Gt. Flute 8′ and soft Mixture)
Gt.
Gt.
f
(Ped.)
(Change A# to:
00 3450 000)
Ch. to Mixture
A#
mf (detached)
Sw. to Oboe
(detached)

Gt.
Gt.
(Sw.)
(reduce B to:
00 3500 000)
Ch. Flute
legato
p Gt. Gamba
Gt.
(Ped.)

Gt.
Gt.
ff
L.H. Solo
F♯ (00 4675 300)
Gt. Flute
D♯ (00 8740 000)
Ch.
Gt.
p

Gt.
Gt.
f
Ped. 16′, 8′
4 - 2
Sw. Trumpet
G♯ (00 6876 540)
Ch. to Mixture
F (00 6644 322)

Gt. Flute and Mixture
Gt.
Gt. Flute 8′
Gt.
Ch. 8′, 2′
B 00 5805 000
(Ped.)
Ped. 16′, 8′

simile

Broadly

SHEEP MAY SAFELY GRAZE

From the Birthday Cantata (No. 208)

"WAS MIR BEHAGT, IST NUR DIE MUNTRE JAGD"

Pipe and Electronic Organs:

Sw. Krummhorn, or other solo stop
Gt. Flute 8′
Pedal 16′, 8′

by

J. S. BACH

Arranged in the Key of G Major by

E. POWER BIGGS

Hammond Registration
by CHESTER KINGSBURY

Sw. A♯ 00 3554 210
Gt. A♯ 00 4501 000
B 00 5613 000
Ped. 3 - 1 Vibrato: OFF
Prepare: Sw. A♯ , Gt. A♯

This Prelude is an arrangement of a Soprano Aria from Cantata No. 208 for the birthday of Duke Christian of Sachzen-Weissenfels in 1716. The fresh, pastoral character of the music is a remarkable instance of Bach's power of tone painting. The phrasing throughout should be on the pattern of the first measures.

Also published for Piano and Organ; and for Organ and Strings. Recorded on Columbia M 30539.

Gt.
Gt.
Sw.
Sw.
Gt.
Gt.
Prep. Sw. F♯
Sw.
Sw.
Ped. 4 - 1

Gt.
Gt.
Sw.
Sw.

Gt.
Gt.
Ped. 3 - 1
Prep. Sw. A♯

simile
Sw.
Sw.

Gt.
Gt.
Sw.
Sw.
Gt.
Gt.

THE SHEPHERDS AT THE MANGER

From the Piano Suite "The Christmas Tree"
composed in 1875-76 and dedicated by Liszt
to his granddaughter, Daniela von Bülow.

Hammond Registration
by CHESTER KINGSBURY

Sw.	A	00 7536 035
	B	00 6005 000
Gt.	A	00 5252 310
	B	00 4203 000
Vibrato:	OFF	

Arranged for Organ by
E. POWER BIGGS

The Music by
FRANZ LISZT

Gt.
reduce Sw.
Gt.
Prep.
Sw. C♯
Sw.
rall.
Sw. A♯
add to Sw.
a tempo
cresc.
Gt. D♯
Ch. Clar.

rall.
a tempo

poco a poco
Sw. B
reduce Sw.
rall.
Sw.
Gt. A♯
Sw. 8', 2'
Reset Gt. B:
00 4000 000
Gt. G♯
Sw. F
Gt. A♯
Sw. C♯
poco a poco rall.
Gt. B

SINFONIA, CHORALE and VARIATION

From the Easter Cantata (No. 4)

"Christ Lay in Death's Dark Prison"

by

JOHANN SEBASTIAN BACH

Arranged for Organ Solo by

E. POWER BIGGS

Hammond Registration
(in Circles and Frames) by
PORTER HEAPS

Sw. (A♯) 33 6646 455
(B) 32 3434 333
Gt. [A♯] 00 7777 554
Pedal 6-4 Vibrato: OFF

Sw. } Diapasons 8′, 4′, 2′ (or String Chorus)
Gt. } Sw. to Gt.
Ped. Diapasons 8′, 4′, 2′

1. Sinfonia

2. Chorale

("Christ Lay in Death's Dark Prison")

Gt. Full, with Mixtures
Ped. Full, with Mixtures

On Hammond, play both hands an octave higher.

3. Variation

("Now Jesus Christ, the Son of God")

Sw. Full, with Mixtures
Gt. Trumpet 8′
Ch. Full, with Mixtures; Sw. to Ch.
Ped. 16′, 8′, 4′

Adagio
Allegro
tr

Ch.
Sw.
rall.
a tempo
rall.

SLOW MOVEMENT
(From "Concerto in D Minor")

by
ANTONIO VIVALDI
(1675-1741)

Sw. Oboe 8′
Ch. soft 8′, 4′
Ped. soft 16′, 8′

Hammond Registration
(in Circles and Frames) by
PORTER HEAPS

Sw. (A) 00 5676 554
(B) 55 6322 111
Gt. [A♯] 00 5432 100
Pedal 4-2 Vibrato 1 (slow)

Edited by
E. POWER BIGGS

Arranged for Organ by
JOHANN SEBASTIAN BACH

A♯
rall.
a tempo
(Echo)
(Ch.)
Ch.
Gt.
rall.

A SOLEMN PRELUDE

"Sighing, Weeping, Sorrow, Need"

From Cantata No. 21 by

J. S. BACH

Arranged for Organ Solo by

E. POWER BIGGS

Sw. Oboe, Salicional and Flute 4′
Ch. Soft Flutes 8′
Ped. 16′, 8′ to Ch.
(Solo Orchestral Oboe if available)

Hammond Registration
(in Frames) by
CHESTER KINGSBURY
Sw. B 00 0760 400
Gt. A♯ 00 4225 000
B 00 3512 000
Pedal 4-2 Vibrato: OFF
Prepare: Sw. B Gt. B

rall.
Gt.
Ch.
Sw.
a tempo
Sw.

Sw. B
Sw. (or Solo Oboe)
rall.
mp a tempo
Ch.
Gt. B
rall.

THE TROPHY

by

FRANÇOIS COUPERIN

Arranged for Organ by

E. POWER BIGGS

HAMMOND REGISTRATION BY
CHESTER KINGSBURY
Sw. A♯ 01 7887 650
Gt. A♯ 00 5646 224
Vibrato: OFF
Prepare: Sw. A♯ Gt. A♯

Sw. Trumpet *f*
Ch. Trumpet *mf*
or 8′, 4′, 2′ ensemble *mf*

Allegretto

Sw.
Sw.
tr
tr
cresc.
6